Alice Through Wonderland

Nandita Banerjee

DEDICATION

For my granddaughter, Saanvi, on her first birthday.

Contents

PREFACE

Alice through Wonderland, an anthology of various types of poems, is inspired by two great works of literature, namely, Lewis Carol's novel, *Alice in Wonderland* (1865) and William Wordsworth's ode, *Intimations of Immortality* (1804). It traces the journey of a girl, Alice, into and through "Wonderland," her childhood in our modern day.

Like Wordsworth's ode, this anthology claims that human souls have their own joyful existence in Heaven before they come to Earth, and when they are born, they bring heavenly perceptions with them.

Little Alice in the anthology sees the everyday world through the lens of her earlier heavenly existence. Like her namesake in Lewis Carol's novel, she meets and interacts with anthropomorphic creatures. However, her experiences in "Wonderland" do not end there. "The world oozes pleasures of her own." Like the other Alice, she gains a deeper understanding of the world through her involvement with its denizens and their activities, while letting go of her childish innocence along the way.

And it is not just her innocence that Alice loses in the anthology. As she grows, the heavenly vision she is born with fades. The routines and habits of daily life set in, and the world goes from looking enchanted to looking "common."

PREEXISTENCE

I live as a soul in Heaven.

WITHIN THE PEARLY GATES

I come into being in his golden hand,
bodiless and free in his golden land,
one of boundless nature,
with many an exotic plant and creature—
clothed in his light,
gleaming bright.

I wander through his gilded forest,
where the divine sunrays come to rest.
In the light that paints them warm,
the trees are in full form.
They dance with amazing ease,
a piece choreographed by the breeze,
and as the leaves sway and move,
a part of me does too—to the groove.

The river glides among forest roots,
calling up to golden boughs and shoots.
She's one of those shakers and movers,
jiving to music—the song of her waters,
drinking in rays so pure,
her dappled whorls and ripples a lure.
There is something about the hues
that sparkle upon the blues.

The mighty mountains catch the light,
dazzle, glow-capped, radiantly bright.
On their slopes, flowers bloom fair,
insects dangle like stars mid-air.
Each bird's a supernal entity
with wings fluttering like confetti.
The clouds above are sweet golden pools,
I wait beneath for a shower of jewels.

Among the blisses galore,
I grow hungry to explore,
when a path leads out

to some place without,
of wonders new,
wild, veiled in dew.

There is no turning back.
I continue along the well-trodden track.

BABYHOOD

The earthbound journey begins.

PAST THE DUE DATE

I was beginning to get weary
of the dullness within the womb,
of crouching in a sac of water,
of having nothing to do.

Deep asleep I seemed to be,
yet I was wide awake,
pining for the buzz without—
that crooning and the gentle laugh.

Oh, to hear those sounds again,
be in that world that made them.
It couldn't be as boring as here.
Things always seemed to happen there.

But was it safe, this land,
of which I had grown so fond,
How'd I know without going outside?
I could not be bound to this sac for life!

The days crawled, slow and dull.
I tossed and turned, whirled around.
What if I stirred up a storm?
Some sort of help would surely come.

Then came those words, impatient,
as though from one in great haste.
"Oh dear! Oh dear! I am late!"
Would things change, now they were said?

The sounds grew loud, somewhat grim.
"Any moment the baby's coming."
Me? All excited, I quaked.
In a moment, down I went.

EARTHBOUND PLIGHT

I rush out
of my home
of nine months,
with not a
thought about
how in the world,
if things didn't
work out,
I am to get back.

The path's bumpy.
Whoa, it dips so
suddenly down.
A tight squeeze.
Am I too big,
or is the passage
too small?
If only it would
stop shaking.
Oh, wow, it's
stretching,
dancing 'mid
whoops and squeals.

The light!
I am falling.
Terrified, I shriek.
They pick me up,
surround me
with so much love.
How sweet they talk.
How warm they feel.
They cuddle me.
I snuggle up.

Is it full of wonders,
this world?

WONDERLAND

Amid all that light and noise
I see Mommy's face, Daddy's too.
How tenderly they cuddle.
I know them, those two.
I've heard them coo to me
as I was growing within Mommy,
deep down in her tummy.

They kiss me for the nth time,
saying, "We love you so."
How hard I try to say it back.
They just smile, like they know.
"You are," they chime, "our very own.
This is the best moment we've known."
Oh, their soft, crooning tone!

They talk about taking me
to a place called "home."
In no time, I am buckled
into a tiny li'l "baby-dome."
Daddy picks me up. I'm all ears.
Mommy mouths, "Careful dears."
Daddy just laughs. "No fears."

Outside, the air is warm and nice,
My eyes scrunch—it's too bright!
Daddy rocks me back and forth,
"It's alright, baby, all alright."
Something sweet fills me within.
"How our baby juts out her chin,"
Mommy sighs. "Taking the scents in?"

Of the many, one. It's in the breeze,
in the air, in the garden full of flowers.
Mommy calls them "gardenias,"
says they've grown a lot in the showers.

Amidst those shapes, dances a gleam,
clothing all in its rosy beam.
I've known it before—in a dream?

NEWBORN BLISSES

The world oozes pleasures of her own—
Mommy and Daddy's love, set in stone,
Big Sis, they call my "forever friend,"
grandparents' cuddles that know no end.

Too happy in my happiness,
and thankful for my luckiness,
I sink into a life of comfort,
cushy-soft and smooth like yogurt.

THE ACT OF CRYING

Just the act of crying
brings them flying—
the entire family.
"Are you hungry, lovely,"
they ask, picking me up.
I show no signs of shutting up.
Oh, the shower of affection,
kisses, and attention.
They fetch me water, they bring me food,
whatever they deem will change my mood.
I feel so precious, safe, and secure,
I'm the most loved baby in the world, I'm sure.

ENDLESS IMITATION

The sweetest sounds stay with me,
the coos and sweet nothings,
words of comfort and of love—
I copy them with my babblings.

Every day, my world grows big.
So much catches my fancy.
I try and mimic them all,
like a li'l chimpanzee.

I fill my make-believe stage,
with every quirk and action,
as if my whole life's work
were endless imitation.

PIGMY-SIZED

The changes are so gentle, I barely
notice them happen.

NATURE IS TO ME ALL IN ALL

The storm roars.
I race out the doors,
leaving behind my plush bear
for the restless air.
The wind tears at my dress,
whips my hair up in a mess.

The black clouds frown,
the rain pours down.
It soaks through.
My clothes stick like glue.
Woo-hoo, I sing,
spin, and swing.

The thunder rumbles,
I jump in puddles,
climb the trees,
scrape my knees,
chase a frog,
race through the fog.

I haven't a clue
when the sky turns blue,
or the sun is shining,
or that Mommy is calling.
Not until I must drag myself in.
If only it wasn't so dry within.

I WISH I WERE OUTSIDE

My home is filled with wonders,
chosen with care by all I know,
anything to keep me squeaky clean,
on days when there's a downpour.

There are these piles of fairy tales.
Mom picks one up—*Rapunzel*.
She begins to read it at once.
Dad happily mimes the actions.

"I wish I were outside," I cry.
"Out in the open, under the skies,
running through the big, dark forest,
picking up daisies and bluebells."

They decide I'll love the Disney film.
Rapunzel blares on the TV screen.
From the couch, I watch the rain,
the drops playing catch on the foggy panes.

A PYGMY-SIZED DARLING

Behold me among
my paints and brushes,
a pigmy-sized darling,
cheered on by sallies
of Mommy's kisses,
buoyed up by the sparkle
in Daddy's eyes!
They're so proud.
They gasp with surprise,
calling the artwork,
a "depiction of life!"
Yet, that gleam,
I create with sequins,
swimming in
gluey blodges,
simply passes them by.

Before long,
I throw that aside,
find Big Sis and
smiling wide,
con another part,
strut about
my make-belief stage,
shouting louder
than thunder,
"Off with your head."
My face turns l red.
Big Sis doesn't look up.
If only she cares.
I may not be
big like her,
but I could still be her friend.

THE WONDER OF TEARS

I wonder at the magic of tears,
drops that no one hears.
I shed a few and help is at hand,
as and when I demand.
It's like they can tell I'm sad.
Yet, they cry even when they are glad.

THE RAINBOW

I gasp at the
rainbow,
that bridge
of colors
over the sea
of gloom.

Oh, the joy!
It seeps into
my bones,
my blood,
my heart,
soul too.

"Just a ray
of light
from the sun,
hitting
a raindrop,"
says Mom.

Her voice!
Does she not
see the magic
of the colors
in the middle
of nowhere?

Does it not
spark a wonder
in her—how
the band sits so
neat among the
messy clouds?

Mom talks
the same way

about every
other joy—
moon, stars,
flower, rain.

Like those
beauties are
no different
from the
baubles
at the store.

I FEEL, I FEEL IT ALL

Grumble, grumble, thunder cloud.
How I wonder how you shroud
the moon and all the stars so high
and jolt your fire through the sky.

Dazzle, dazzle, big, red sun.
I wonder how you are so fun,
perched among clouds so high,
cheering each day that goes by.

Glimmer, glimmer, silver moon.
How do you, you li'l balloon,
shed so much light from up so high.
Queen of the star-spangled sky!

Shimmer, shimmer, bow of colors.
Wonder how you outdo all others,
line up all your pretty ribbons so high,
and bridge the gap 'twixt earth and sky?

EATING TOGETHER

The table is set for four,
with silverware, plates, and bowls.
Dinnertime is special—we eat together.

I smell the garden,
simmering in Mom's vegetable soup.
She chews ice cubes—they keep her cool.

Dad has meat—well-done,
brown and dry with no juices at all.
He likes asparagus—on the side.

Big Sis must have her veggies,
fish, and all things healthy.
She's a growing girl—she's seventeen.

I stuff myself with chips and puds,
and I am always excused.
I'm only li'l—just five.

MY SECRET FRIENDS

My friends, Star and Suzie,
I've known them for years.
They come and play with me,
most of my walking hours.

Mom can't see them.
Actually no one can.
Does it really matter?
We have so much fun.

With them I don't decide
what to play—we just know.
I never want them to lose,
but they do anyhow.

It all goes well until
Big Sis catches me boxing
my own ears for cheating myself,
in some silly match.

She always watches me play
and says she finds it queer,
why I pretend to be two,
and sometimes three people.

ANIMALS GALORE

Animals are great listeners—I can share my
secrets and thoughts with them, and they will tell no one.

THIS WORLD OF ANIMALS

Among my friends, is every li'l animal,
real, magical, fantastical—
long-tailed rats,
playful cats,
not to speak of caterpillars
that smoke hookahs behind pillars.
Well, they do at the bookstore,
where between the covers, lions roar
as do the loud gryphons,
hodge-podge creatures with talons.

In this land there's animals galore,
some as old as the dinosaur,
for instance, the silly old dodos.
You just get to see them in photos!
Anyway, I love animals that snuggle,
with twinkling eyes and a gentle nuzzle.

THE CHESHIRE CAT

Dinah, my cat, is such a dear.
He's always grinning from ear to ear.
If he finds me upset,
at once he'll get all set
to brighten my day with joy and cheer.

THE DORMOUSE

The dormouse crouches there on that brick,
listening to the clock go tick, tock, tick.
Hours go by, he stays still,
statue-like until,
he hears "cat" and is all panic.

THE CATERPILLAR

The caterpillar changes too fast
into all kind of forms that do not last—
now an egg, now larva,
now silky—the pupa,
and then, a butterfly in skies so vast.

PETS ARE THE BEST

Pets are the best,
in whatever shape.
Hug them,
talk to them,
show them respect,
and you will find,
you know their language.

YEARNING TO GROW

The world does all she can to make me forget the glories I have known.

TINY LI'L ME

I love Mom's handbags and shoes,
dresses, and makeup—
"brand names" she calls them.
How long must I wait to be like her?
Years rush by, I barely get bigger.

I drool over Big Sis's high heels—
not to mention her sports sedan.
Oh, her "prized possessions!"
Eighteen's such a lovely age to be,
unlike six. Wee li'l me!

I'm quite tired of being so tiny,
with my pygmy desk, pygmy bed, pygmy—
I want to grow big and mighty,
act of my own free will.
If only there was a "drink me" potion or pill!

WHITE LIES

I open my mouth,
and out pops a whopper.
The third this year!

Big Sis calls them my grandiose fibs!
Yet, they're pretty harmless,
just me trying to impress.

I try to smile as I speak,
though my voice sounds a bit strange.
"It's just a phase," says Mom. "She will change."

"She recycles my stories," Big Sis complains.
Do I? If only I had her life, and she mine,
I would not live with her, but float on cloud nine!

MY CAREFREE LIFE

I rush back from school and
tumble into my playland—
my snug, sun-drenched den—
run around in circles when,
a book catches my eye.
Big Sis's? I must read it, at least try.
My heart and mind are not my own,
but like the pieces of fairy tales strewn
all over my cluttered li'l den.
I race out with the find into the garden.

There I slump down by the brook,
whip through the pages of the book.
Alas, there are no pictures,
not one between the covers.
It's one of those books to be ignored.
Who could read it without getting bored?
Grown-ups to be sure.
They're um, what's the word? Mature?

The brook gushes in the lively breeze,
"Atishoo!" I sneeze, but not freeze.
On a whim, I dip my feet in the water.
It soaks my shoes—all that pretty leather.
Eeks! I run indoors,
where everyone's busy, doing their chores.

Mom and Dad are on "Google."
There is a bottle on the breakfast table.
Some grown-up drink?
I will chug it down before they blink.
Who cares about what happens after?
I can barely hold back my laughter.

I gulp it down and my eyelids droop.
My head throbs at the smell of soup.
That's Big Sis stirring liquid food—

mushy peas in gravy—snotty hued.
A book waits by her side for when she's done.
When I'm all grown up, I will write one.

IF I WERE ALL GROWN-UP

"Grandma," I said, "you're so beautiful
and wonderfully tall.
Tell me, how you got to that height.
I just hate being so small."

"When I was your age," replied she,
"I was tiny as an elf,
but I exercised daily, rested, ate well—
I took good care of myself."

"Grandma," I said, "I run and I skip.
I sleep eight hours and eat like a pig.
I don't shoot up. Is there no magic pill
for quickly growing big?"

Grandma peered over her glasses at me.
"Your genes are the major determinant
of exactly how tall you will be.
Still, you must eat healthy—that's important."

"Eat healthy?" I stared at her in disbelief.
"Do you mean the mushy peas and slimy leeks,
or is it the sour fruit on the dinner table?
Do you have any idea how that stuff reeks?"

"Reeks!" Grandma snorted. "Mandarins!
Have them regularly, and you're free of disease.
And you must, of course, remember your vitamins.
Now thrash those candies and have some fruit, please."

She noticed the bulge in my pocket! Her eyes!
Some stuff she ate as a child? No doubt bland.
Unwillingly, I gave up my pops for the bitter fruit.
If I was all grown up, I could've ignored her command.

INSIDE MY HEAD

In my wonderful and absurd dreams, wishes, and imaginings, I
find a balance between nonsense and reason.

IN MY WACKY WORLD

I chase a talking rabbit
into a wacky world,
It is just my curious spirit
so eager to learn
about the li'l creatures,
that one sees in pictures,
waiting to entertain me,
with their wit and whimsy.

I chat up a turtle,
insult a mouse,
run a race—
circle the place,
freak out when the
caterpillar asks
like at an exam
who I am.
I am changing
every month . . .
I don't know.
Oh!

I invite myself to a hare's tea party,
where the guests are positively nutty.
They bombard me with riddles,
unanswerable—the sort that muddles.

I befriend
a deck of cards
with legs that walk,
and mouths that talk,
play croquet,
use flamingoes
as mallets.
Devouring cutlets,
the Queen-o'-Hearts
strikes the balls—

hedgehogs that roll
out of control.

In the heart of Wonderland,
the creatures are mouthy,
not to mention, blooming mad—
the way they think and act.
And as for reasoning, few will.
They would rather chill
unlike humans. That's who I am—
must tell the caterpillar. Pure bedlam!

MY VERY OWN FROG PRINCE

I am beginning
to get tired of
behaving myself
at this sit-down dinner,
with little to do,
save eating
flat-tasting food,
while listening to
Chopin and Mozart.

The hot day
makes me sleepy.
I stifle a yawn,
find joy in
the statue of a frog.
There's a
purrrreeeek.
A frog's stuttering trill?
Did one just run past?
I take off at once,
catch a glimpse.
He looks strikingly
like the one in the film.
If only I could kiss him
back to being a prince.
My very own . . .

He leaps headlong
into the neighbor's pond,
shadowy in the light
of the setting sun,
then turns up
on a lily pad.
The neighbor's watching,
but I jump on.
My frog prince looks sad,
his croak sounds hoarse.

I hug him quick,
but before we kiss,
the pad's gone.
We sink down
to the bottom.
Ker-plunk.

"Wake up, sleepyhead!"
my neighbor yells.
Phew! I jump
out of my skin.
She is at my table!
The statue grins
from its stand
There was no adventure
in the lily-pond.

I WISH

Wish I was born with some special blessing,
such that in my garden, a fairy would be tenting,
with a slender wand to swish
and grant my ev'ry li'l wish.
And on my sixteenth birthday,
she would lead me away,
through the arbor in the garden,
where shadows darken,
to a palace green.
There a prince would dub me queen.

In that palace I would reign forevermore,
only yards from Mommy and Daddy's door.

AN INTERESTING TRADITION

I lost a baby incisor,
dropped it in a mouse hole,
as I was bid,
for a strong mousey tooth.

I never saw any mouse,
though the next morning,
I felt a solid bump
under my pillow.

It was a pouch
with a five-dollar bill
and a note saying, "Thanks!"
Was it from the mouse?

Mommy said she saw wings,
guessed they were visiting fairies.
But I gave them nothing.
Did the mouse give them my tooth?

OPINIONS DIFFER

"Dinah's my cat,"
I say to the rat.
"She's a dear ball of fur,
so soft—you'd like that.
Why on earth do you shiver?'

"Felines are," she mutters,
"double-faced tormentors.
My family hates pets like that,
runs a mile from those slaughterers.
Never, never trust a cat!"

"But Dinah's a cute, li'l thing,
so sweet and caring.
We couldn't be closer,
and she's the best at catching—"
The rat is bristling all over.

Oh, no! "I beg your pardon!"
I cry when,
trembling down to the end of her tail,
the rat flees into her den,
I beg her to return, but to no avail.

THE LONG SAD TALE

I get down on my knees,
toss some cheese
down the rat hole.
I want to cajole
her out, but she is not around.
In fact, she is not to be found.
I search carefully, yet she
is unnoticeable, crouched under the settee.
Hours pass and I hear her scratch and gnaw
I crawl in with a kind smile. "Aww!
What are you doing in here?"
"Hiding from your cat. He'll kill me, I swear.
Mine is a long, sad tale."
I feel the swish of her tail.
It is long no doubt—
I frown at the tears on her snout—
but why sad? I keep puzzling,
while she continues, shuffling,
like something's seriously amiss.
So, my idea of her tale is something like this.

Dinah's mad
that you bring
grand feasts
into my hole.
He's greedy,
the vulgar soul,
prone to bouts
of wrath and
jealousy. Can't
believe he pounced on
my tail and gnawed it.
Now it hurts like hell.
Anyways, I had better
shut up for he has
threatened me not to
tell you or else he'll
bite my tail off, make
it look like there
never was one.
I would reta-
liate, go to
court. He
said if I
dared, he
would en-
sure I was
dead
well
before.
How
do I
deal
with
this
rogue?

SCHOOL

At last!
My heart pounds,
I've been waiting for this day.

HAPPY AT SCHOOL

Some say shades of the prison house begin to
close on me. School's a prison? Not true!
I love my school—it's the best place ever. Ooh!

I love the teacher's smile, my classroom,
the pictures, toys, and the bookroom—
"the library"—by the patio where flowers bloom.

I make new friends, give them nicknames.
The teacher takes pictures while we play games.
Our faces are locked up in picture frames.

We become forever friends—li'l angels,
who can at will, turn into devils.
We are all good at numbers and puzzles.

We learn about the life cycle, make a display.
I now know so many nice, big words to say
that often blow Mommy and Daddy away.

Anyway, I must rush, dress pretty.
Tonight, Gran turns eighty.
I'm a special guest at her birthday party.

POOLS ARE COOL

No longer do I splash around in a puddle
with Joel, like we are in a muddle.
Now we swim in the humongous pool,
cool and welcoming, at the school.

The coach shows us difficult ways to dive.
He tells us we'll survive,
that learning a new dive is never easy—
it can make us feel a little queasy.

I plunge headlong into the water.
Accidentally, I knock Joel over.
"I don't like water in my eyes,"
thrashing around the pool, he cries.

"Oh, I beg your pardon—all my fault."
I apologize while trying to somersault.
The water surges up and drenches my friend.
He springs out of the pool, all red.

"Oh, I beg your pardon!" I repeat.
"It's okay." Joel smiles sweet.
He jumps back into the waters blue.
I splash and kick; he does too.

The coach teaches the forward flip.
I can't believe we get a grip.

THE LOBSTER QUADRILLE

We danced the Lobster Quadrille,
from *Alice in Wonderland* at school.
We practiced until we mastered the skill.
Honestly, it was so cool.
The backdrop of the seashore,
comprising seals, squids and crabs galore,
was painted by us, Grade Four.

Dressed like the creatures in the sea,
how eagerly we partnered,
with lobsters in a spree,
danced, cartwheeled, and capered,
screaming and shouting wildly,
tail treading the whitings slyly,
ousting the shellfish finally.

MAKE A GUESS

My first is in fairy but not in princess.
My second is in angel, not in empress.
My third is in pelican and also in parrot.
My fourth is in mango, but never in carrot.
My fifth is in ice, not in blue.
My sixth is second in uncle, and first when in new.
My seventh is in piggy, soggy, and baggy twice.
My last is in doldrum as well as in concise.

What am I?

THE SPELLING TEST

The spelling test was about to begin.
I picked up my pencil, saw Joel grin.
"Omniscient," was the first word.
"I know that one," said the nerd.
He wrote "omnishent." "That's wrong," I said.
He didn't correct it but scoffed instead.
"I, make mistakes?" He seemed ready for combat.
"I always score full marks, unlike you. You know that."

"Number two," the teacher called, "'mischievous.'"
Joel wrote m-i-s-c-h-e-i-v-o-u-s.
Then showed it off. "See, right as rain."
"Wrong, again." I saw his smile wane.
"I've never been wrong, Alice, not yet,
though it's a shame you don't get
that I'm better than you at this." He spat.
"I always score full marks, unlike you. You know that."

"You're overconfident, Joel, you didn't practice."
At this point the teacher walked past. "Anything amiss?"
I shifted in my seat, sensing trouble.
"Not at all," I heard Joel mumble.
He was moved to the next row.
The test resumed; the teacher moved away, kind of slow.
"Do not doubt my spelling skills," said the brat.
"I always score full marks, unlike you. You know that."

The test was over. I got my score—
Twenty-four out of twenty-four!
Joel was quiet, kind of evasive.
I tried talking to him, but he was defensive.
And his face was white as a sheet.
"I ran out of time. I um, didn't complete.
I'm good at spelling." His voice was flat.
"I always score full marks. Unlike most. You know that."

TOO BIG OR TOO LI'L

An intriguing question—does anyone know
the answer?

A FULL-BLOWN TANTRUM

I was yards from Joel's house
when I heard the noise.
I crept up, quiet as a mouse,
and recognized his voice.
Meltdown over toys?
They get away with everything—boys!

"Joel?" I knocked on his door.
It opened, a plate flew out, almost hitting my nose.
Angry footsteps strutted across the floor.
"Joel!" I ventured in on tiptoes.
"He's anxious about schoolwork," said his mother,
picking up pieces of his spelling book, strewn all over.

There were traces of pickle too, on the floor and staircase.
"Joel," I called. "Can you please explain what's going on?"
He emerged with a tear-blotched face.
"It's the pickle in my lunch," he said with a yawn.
"Mom put too much." He laughed, rocking his locks.
How did the pickle find its way out of his lunchbox?

BIZARRE OPTIMISM

If I had a world of my own,
it would be different from every place known.
It would be as hot and cold as I please.
Rain would pour at ease
from rainbow skies,
its temperature as required—a pleasant surprise
in sunshine, moonshine, and snowfall,
each droplet, a fragrance ball.

If I had a world of my own,
it would be in some magical zone.
The sea would be within easy reach,
and every town, have its own beach.
Sea foam would swirl into icy cream and
run into waffle cones, the color of sand.

If I had a world of my own,
every town would be known
for its exclusive breakfast menu of joys.
Every resident would be allowed a choice
of their own daily pleasures.
Stringent measures
would be in place, so sadness and foes
could never venture close—
happiness would reset itself in a tall tower
with every passing hour.

A BIT FAR-FETCHED

Joel sailed the seas on a ship,
he had stories to tell of his trip,
of some weird animal he had seen
in the fantastical land he had been.
"It was queer," he said, "with a pearly horn,
yet so like the horse-like animal—the unicorn."
"Found throughout mythologies," I hissed.
"But you don't see them—they don't exist."
He sighed. "But I saw one that set the snow
in the deep, dark forest aglow,
and the light healed a sick girl—"
He twirled a curl.
"Really? Where is she?" asked I.
"She ran off." He evaded my eye.
"How about you cruise across the Atlantic.
The scenes, believe me, are simply majestic."

BIG OR LI'L

I'm too li'l to have my very own bank card,
my closest friends do, and I find it hard.
I'm too li'l to go anywhere without permission
or have a say in every family decision.
Big Sis does and can go to the mall alone.
I'm not allowed that or even a phone.

Yet, I'm too big to whine
when I'm out to dine,
to raise my voice,
to make merry or rejoice,
and should I break into tears,
I'm reminded of my years.

I wish I was still three.
Fifty-three inches is a wretched height to be.
Mostly, I'm off what they call their "radar,"
and when I am on, every word I utter
is noise to their ears.
Yet they say, losing me is the worst of their fears.

TELLING OFFS

The adults in my life seem to change
their attitude as I grow older. Strange!
There are consequences for actions
when there are so many distractions,
telling offs for having a li'l fun.
Last night there was one,
about a burner phone in my bookcase.
I kind of felt I needed my space.
Now who would respect that?
None, except Dinah, my cat.

I hid in the unused attic.
A li'l dramatic?
Well, revenge is sweet.
For hours, I heard panicked feet,
constant bickering, rows, and wails.
I listened to every argument, the details
of how they'd been too severe,
that I was "such a dear,"
the best child by far of all they'd known.
I heard Mom sob and sadly moan.

Organized search began.
What was my plan?
Alas, I didn't have one.
And it was no longer fun.

I crawled out of the attic space,
watched Mom wipe her face.
I called her from the landline, tried to talk.
"Like Big Sis, I'm out for a walk—"
She gasped. "Come right back. Quick!
I have been worried sick.
You're too young; your sister's twenty-one.
You shouldn't have left without telling anyone—"
She broke into sobs only yards from me.
I ran into her arms, crying, "Missed you so much, Mommy."

STILL A CHILD

In another year, I shall be ten.
How different will I be then?
Already I comply with every rule.
What a lot they teach at school.
Especially that deadly Mrs. Red,
with her "Off with your head."
How easy it is to offend her.
Mistakes stick in her brain like burr.
Despite my pleadings, I'm never excused,
and she sees to it that the matter's not diffused.
Parents are called in—oh, her vicious tongue!
No one seems to remember that I'm still quite young.

THE CENSOR IN MY HEAD

There's this person in my head,
a worldly-wise friend I dread,
controlling my emotions,
my actions, and reactions,
prompting nonstop,
going over the top.
Despite, I stumble, glance around, praying,
that people staring, might not be saying,
"A great girl like you, Alice,
to be walking like this!"

The person in my head condemns me.
"Honestly, Alice, can't you see?"
My face is wet with tears,
the worst of my fears.
I trip and fall on the pavement.
"Great accomplishment!"
The internal sermon grows so loud,
I rise, pull myself out of the crowd.
My tears dripping, I stand up tall.
The censor demands I forget the fall.

GROWTH SPURTS

The mini growth spurts
are fast and furious until the really big one hits.

GROWING UP

I'm growing more and more.
I can barely squeeze in through my playroom door.
All my clothes have become too tiny to wear,
yet, I do not despair.
I so needed this growth spurt,
it was beginning to hurt.
It's such a treat, my brand-new wardrobe—
denim, tees, jackets, leggings, bathrobe.

Though this growth spurt's been a bit too sudden,
it didn't come unbidden.
Overnight life's full of incredible possibilities,
new and challenging responsibilities.
I have grown more response-able,
efficient and reliable,
can do jobs promptly that need getting done,
even regular chores. I make them fun.

THE LONG TUNNEL

Life runs along, along a long tunnel.
There are rigid walls, straight lines,
and everything's predictable.

Life runs along, along a long tunnel.
Daily routines constrict my life.
I crave adventure.

Life runs along, along a long tunnel.
Books loom, full of information.
Hardly any have pictures.

Life runs along, along a long tunnel.
Somewhere in all that rigidity,
I glimpse slippery tracks.

Life runs along, along a long tunnel.
I slip and swim, jounce and glide,
in the li'l chaos.

LURE OF TECHNOLOGY

It was a crisp spring day,
in the month of May,
I leaned against the windowsill,
watching liquid sunshine spill
from duck egg blue skies.
What a feast for the eyes!

Mom came in with crackers and cheese.
"Mom," I cried, "please,
may I have a smartphone?"
"Smartphone?" she spoke in a weird tone.
Is it the cost?
"To um," I said, "ensure I never get lost,
you know, when I go for a walk?
You could call—we could talk.
My friends do that—"
"If they're not," Mom mumbled, "in group chat."

"Group chat" sounds fun.
I've never been invited to one.
I don't have a phone; I don't fit in.
My smile wore thin.
"Mom, you talk like one of those families
that are real-life tragedies,
where kids aren't allowed to watch TV,
other than the occasional family movie.
I use the computer, the net.
When did Big Sis get—?"
"When," Mom muttered, "she was thirteen.
We, as parents, aren't really mean."

A jay dove down to my window from the sky.
Why here? It can fly.
I marveled at its beauty. Fairy kind.
Mom stared at me like she read my mind.
"How about getting your homework done?
Then we could do something fun.

Like play games on your Nintendo 3DS."
I nodded at the game console. "I guess."

ADVENTUROUS TASTEBUDS

Mom's friend from Maine gave her
the recipe for a special chowder—
to be cooked thick and hearty with clams,
bacon, and the finest hams.

Mom browned the bacon, and made it crisp
with old-fashioned butter, just a wisp,
then added clams and hams with slushy cream,
for the chowder to taste like a dream.

Beau—ootiful Soo—oop!
Who would not stoop to scoop
this creamy soup—soup of the evening,
fresh in the tureen, gently simmering?

SHOWING OFF

"Important—unimportant—important,"
Big Sis muttered under her breath,
then let out a sigh. "Not that it signifies much."
Wow! How grown-up she sounds!
Not like me with my limited vocabulary.
I must go more often to the library.

"Getting awfully near graduation,"
I said, with a mighty toss of my head.
Not like I was sure what "graduation" meant,
but it was a nice, grand word to use to impress,
as well as a reminder of the end-of-ELEM ceremony.
Big Sis had bragged about her high school prom to me!

"Your elementary school graduation?"
she barked. "That's not for another two years."
"A year and a month." I swallowed hard.
How I hated the glint in her gaze.
At least I'd used the right word,
not something totally out of context or absurd.

LEARNING TO THINK AND REASON

I begin to see the world differently.

WEIRD ILLOGICAL LINE OF REASONING

Mom labors to bake me that cake,
soft, velvety, purely decadent.
One bite, and I abandon her with my share.
The moral of it is that
appreciating the fruits of labor
makes one selfish.

Two very different reactions,
however mild or balmy wild,
can spring from the same emotion.
So, the moral of that is,
as long as the feeling is the same,
it doesn't matter how one expresses oneself.

We go through life with a sense of purpose,
do the right things, then find that our actions
are prompted by habit, which makes us slaves.
The moral of this is,
if one makes a conscious decision to do what is wrong,
one is a free person, not a machine-like drone.

SO MUCH HAS CHANGED

I emerged from my room dripping wet,
sweating and tearful, all upset.
Mom did not even look up
from the scalding tea in her cup.
Dad squinted at my eyes so red.
"Pull yourself together," he said.
Oh, sullen day!
Sniveling I moved away,
and who should I see, but Big Sis.
"Can't believe you're crying like this!"
she hissed. "Soon there'll be a pool all round,
four inches deep on the ground."
Suddenly, I wished I had not cried so much.
No one had any sympathy as such.

It is so strange,
how things can change
so much in a matter of years.
I'm still young—I can't help my tears.

A PUZZLING QUESTION

Questions return to bombard my mind,
I've tried before to answer the kind,
The answers change over time I find.
One such question is—who am I?
Whatever I say is a lie,
and I must constantly justify.

I am growing every day,
changing in every way.
even my moods—anyway!
I wish none of my teeth were missing,
my hair misbehaving,
or my body hair thickening . . .

Who is this everchanging "me?"
People I'd rather not be:
Mollie, Hollie, at times Natalie.
Mollie cries too easily.
Hollie's rude—the bully!
And Natalie is just silly.

Desperate, I complain.
All my complaints are in vain.
No one has time to listen, despite the pain.
"It's a phase," hisses Big Sis.
"Accept the way it is, miss.
You are and always will be Alice."

NATURE IS NOT WHAT IT USED TO BE

I am on a scavenger hunt
with friends on the river front.
The first question is:
What's the building with the most stories? I whizz
around and see a mansion painted ivory.
The library!
I take a picture, stumbling into flower beds.
Before me a rose garden spreads.
I do not stop but frown at the mention
of a "structure" in the next question:
A bridge that awes.
It carries the path to the land of Oz.
The rainbow? I glance at the horizon,
where the sun is beginning to brighten,
and a band of colors arches into the dreary sky.
A beauty, yet I know not why,
it does not touch my heart,
except as an example of great art,
accomplished by a divine artistic hand.
I click my camera and race down the strand.
The next riddle leads me down to the water's edge.
Row of bushes. Hedge?

THIS SWEET MAY-MORNING

Earth herself is celebrating
this sweet May-morning
with fresh bright flowers,
running riot in bowers,
while the sun shines warm,
and the baby leaps up on his mother's arm,
cooing his "aahs" and "oohs"
at the many colors and vibrant hues.

A pretty picture it is to me,
though I cannot rejoice in the jubilee.
That time is past, the aching joys no more,
but other gifts are in store,
a happier mood, just beholding nature,
sweet sensations, and subdued pleasure.

CURIOUSER & CURIOUSER

Life gets more curious and increasingly strange. I try to make sense of what I see, feel, and hear.

TORTOISE

I am curious about middle school.
Big Sis says, "It was cool.
Mrs. Sawyer tortoise Literature.
She was old and fuzzy like a caterpillar.
Mrs. Rome tortoise History.
Thanks to her, the old eras are a mystery.
Mrs. Bone tortoise Biology.
She was a novice with technology.
Mr. Haiti tortoise Geography.
He led his class to catastrophe.
Mrs. Flintstone tortoise—"
"You make me nauseous,"
I interrupt. "Why tortoise?"
"Because they tortoise," says she. "Taught us."

STRANGE FACTS

Your pinky is the strongest finger.
A day on Venus is longer than a year.

A human heart can beat outside the body as well.
There's a town in Norway called Hell.

Your brain starts slowing down at twenty-four.
It takes nineteen minutes to fall from the North Pole to Earth's
core.

Football teams wearing red kits play better.
The Eiffel Tower gets taller in the summer.

Twins smell the same.
Maine is the only state with a single-syllable name.

Earwax is made of sweat.
Parts of Canada are to the south of Detroit.

The same part of the brain reacts to both happiness and fear.
The Dead Sea is sinking at a rate of about a meter per year.

Strange facts sound like impossibilities,
but truth is not obliged to stick to possibilities.

FOODS IMPACT PERSONALITY

They say hormones
affect our temperament,
but I've read on the internet
that it is not always the case.

Pepper makes us irritable,
vinegar makes us sour,
red meat makes us irrational,
and candies, sweethearts.

Fruits and veggies energize us,
yogurt calms our nerves,
fish helps us concentrate,
and white rice makes us dull.

CURIOSITY

Locked doors,
my curiosity soars.
What's within?
I must get in.

I cannot find the key.
They've hidden it from me.
But why?
I sigh.
Grown-ups are intriguing.
They want us to learn, just not everything.

I cannot tear myself away.
I try to break in all day,
with no success.
I am a mess.
What are they keeping from me?
The thought makes me feel clammy,
and that mighty padlock, furious.
Why make the secret so obvious?

OFF WITH YOUR HEAD

The two wonders of my school
are the disciplinarian, Mrs. Red,
with her "off with your head."
How dreadfully savage!
Then there's the class tattletale—
Gale.
The first never forgives and never forgets.
Her informant never regrets his part.
Apparently, both have our best interests at heart.

TEA PARTY GONE MAD

I organized a li'l tea party, today at three.
Everyone came—everyone who knows me.
It got crowded. Did I call so many? I doubted.
Everyone shouted,
except Elsie, Lacie, and Tilly who fell asleep.
"Twinkle, twinkle, twinkle—" they sang in their sleep,
kind of non-stop.
We had to pinch them to make them stop.
They awoke and pleaded, "Let's not quibble."
"Well then," I said, "sit up and nibble."
"Of course." Together we devoured the treats—
savories and sweetmeats.
We even pretended to have wine,
out of milk jugs in the bright sunshine,
until Joel upset his drink onto his plate,
drew all manner of things on it as he ate,
among them, a raven most grotesque.
"How," he asked, "is this bird like a writing desk?"
I kept guessing like the rest.
Joel was far from impressed.
"Your nose is too small." He eyed it curiously.
"That's outright rude," I replied furiously.
"What do people call a person with no nose like you?"
He chuckled. "Not a clue."

The party continued,
despite the remarks, irrelevant and rude,
spills, chaos, and contempt.
The tea party was no failed attempt.

EVERYONE IS MAD HERE

Everyone is mad here.
Madness is normal.

We shed tears of happiness,
groan at our own delight,
giggle so much when nervous,
the laughter is uncontrollable,
and tears roll down our eyes.

Early on, we're taught to heed
what we share and with whom.
Yet, I'm always in the public eye,
my every movement scrutinized.
Thanks to Mom's Facebook posts.

Adults say it's wrong to lie,
that lies come back to bite us.
Yet, they themselves lie outright,
bend the truth to save their pride,
not to mention their jobs and lives.

THIS SUDDEN INTENSE FEELING

There's this new boy, Hatter,
in the grade below.
He invited me to his tea party,
just as I said "Hello."

I went kind of reluctantly,
whimsical as he was.
His flair for composing riddles,
earned him a big applause.

There's something about the boy
that makes him an enchanter.
Is it his wit or humor?
Not like he's grown any cuter.

We barely know each other.
In fact, we've only just met.
Already, I dream of marrying him
and running off into the sunset.

Here comes Hatter.
Oh! this mad rush
of butterflies in my stomach.
Is this just a crush?

YOUNG TEENAGER

I'm a teen in this day and age.

NOSTALGIA

The rain falls in blinding sheets,
all day long upon forlorn streets,
lightning creeps from cloud to cloud,
thunder rolls in, deafening loud.

I adjust the window blinds.
Down below, a joyful child reminds
me of my wild ecstasies in nature,
of many an unremembered pleasure.

The pictures in my mind revive again
when doe-like, I bounded over hill and plain,
wherever nature led me in my innocence.
They do not restore to me the power of sense.

How unfair that the gleam so bright
should be snatched forever from my sight.
It's no recompense, these new wonders—
Macs, drones, and PS4 players.

They are merely distractions of a kind,
feeding the wayward mind,
triggering negative feelings,
greed, competitiveness, all such things.

The fever of this life divorced from nature!
A walk in the woods is still full of pleasure—
aromas, birdsong, the occasional rabbit,
the dance of the greens to settle the spirit.

THE DREAM THAT IS WONDERLAND

Things always seemed to happen there.
However mild or balmy wild.
Endless imitation.

Dazzle, dazzle big, red sun.
Rainbow skies.
Everyone is mad here.
A bit far-fetched.
My secret friends.

Tea party gone mad.
Happiness would reset itself in a tall tower.
A full-blown tantrum.
This sweet May morning.

I feel, I feel it all.
Strange facts.

Who am I?
Off with your head!
Nature is to me all in all.
Dinah, my cat, is such a dear.
Exclusive breakfast menu of joys.
Raven most grotesque.
Lobster quadrille.
Adventurous tastebuds.
Nostalgia.
Daily routines constrict my life.

ABOUT THE AUTHOR

NANDITA BANERJEE grew up in India and now lives in Houston. With degrees in English Literature and Education, she spent years teaching in India, in the US and in the UK.

In 2011 she decided to give up teaching in favor of a career as a writer. She writes in the supernatural genre and her two-book series No.7 is out on Amazon.

In B' tween:
The Wisp

Nandita Banerjee

Banerjee's magical realism makes for immersive storytelling that demands readers' attention, with dense reality and mysticism blurring into a swirling drama of ghosts, curses, forbidden love, betrayal, and hidden agendas.
The draftsmanship of this character-rich read is impressive, as is the world-building and scene-setting. The novel is wholly inventive from the start, for a read that is singularly original, and richly emotional. Steeped in cultural tradition and the existential desire for salvation, this is a visionary and dramatic piece of contemporary literature... *Self-Publishing Review*

Thoughts
Recollected
In Tranquility

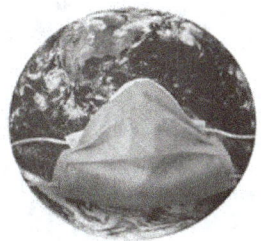

Nandita Banerjee

Upbeat and direct messages about one woman's journey through
the Covid-19 era.
While acknowledging the pandemic's hardships, Banerjee's poems
also effectively articulate battles fought on inner terrain… Political
polarization and conspiracy theories are absent from the
experiences chronicled here; the poet instead favors optimism:
"We've been caught off guard by a thousand unwelcome
circumstances— / it is a supreme act of will staying positive"
("Feelings"). These spare, direct poems are heartfelt, reading more
like aphorisms or microconfessions, resisting elaborate forms in
favor of simple vulnerability... *Kirkus Reviews*

A deeply intimate and probing novel. The prose is lyrical and lush, vacillating between stark, declarative moments of strong prose to thought provoking descriptions and minor self-reflections. *No. 7: The Date* is an exquisitely penned book, demonstrating great draftsmanship and the ability to blend fictional levity and wonder with hard-hitting commentary and relatable characters. Fans of magical realism, character-driven drama, and supernatural thrillers alike will find all the boxes ticked in Banerjee's latest offering...
Self-Publishing Review

No. 7: They're Calling

Nandita Banerjee

No. 7: They're Calling is a stirring supernatural thriller that is rich in detail and widely relatable thanks in large part to carefully crafted and authentic protagonists who never fail to surprise, and a story brimming with unique mystery … *Self-Publishing Review*

www.ingramcontent.com/pod-product-compliance
Lightning Source LLC
Chambersburg PA
CBHW060326130626
46553CB00003B/934